Therapist's Guide to
I Am a Survivor

Purpose of This Workbook

This workbook is a tool for working with children who have survived tra[...] natural disasters, fires, or explosions. It is designed to help clients recall p[...] tions which could result in posttraumatic reactions, and to facilitate the working through and integration of the disaster experiences and its aftereffects. Children who survive such critical events are likely to be significantly affected.

Using the Workbooks

The Growth and Recovery Workbooks are an adjunct to the therapist's work and are not meant to provide the whole therapeutic content. Each therapist brings to the process his or her own originality, creativity, and successful professional experience. It is hoped that the therapist will freely adapt the tasks and activities in the Workbooks to his or her own style and approach, using other materials and activities when appropriate.

Clients should also move at their own pace, and therapists should pursue those topics and modalities most appropriate for each client without being limited by the Workbook format. For instance, with less verbally oriented children the use of art therapy or audio or video cassette recorders may be recommended; certain exercises may be conducted in groups; certain activities may benefit from the presence or involvement of parents or other significant adults who shared in the experience.

Personalizing the approach further ensures that clinical decisions regarding Workbook tasks are dictated by the therapeutic relationship, the individual's level of development, past history of trauma or conflicts, and current circumstances. If a child finds a task too hot to approach, the therapist can choose to return to it later. When something is fruitful it can be pursued with extended tasks, and when a task is neutral the work can move on quickly.

The content of the Workbooks should be shared with parents or significant adults only when the child feels ready for it and if it is therapeutically wise.

Although this series of Workbooks is primarily written for school age children, the tasks are adaptable for use with younger children and adolescents.

Design of the Workbooks

Where possible, a pair of facing pages in the Workbook provides the focus for a complete therapeutic "movement." Depending upon the pacing of the therapy, either a single page or facing pages could provide the material for a session. However, according to the needs of the child, more than one such movement could be made in a single session or several sessions may be devoted to a single movement.

The therapist is always free to select activities in an order appropriate to the client. However, the succession of exercises through the book follows a therapeutically logical progression:

- The initial exercises focus on building the therapeutic alliance.

- The child is then led to relating an overview of the experience.

- This is deepened by a "sensory unpacking" of the experience designed to access and recover traumatic memories. This progression follows a debriefing format, and focuses upon the child's reactions to the incident.

- Delayed reactions are dealt with, and resources are explored.

- Finally, the experience is integrated into the child's whole life experience through a series of strength building exercises.

The Workbook facilitates the survivor's attempt to integrate the traumatic event as an experience of growth. The tasks are process-oriented in that the child's approach to the work, as well as the content information offered, give the therapist important information about the child's defenses, limitations, and strengths.

Summary

The principles of critical incident stress management form the basis for the Growth and Recovery Workbooks. Reviewing and retelling the tale of trauma, feeling and expressing emotional reactions, reduces the child's anxiety, allowing the therapist to help correct misconceptions and balance perspective. The Workbook guides the child through introductory tasks to issues of conflict and concern, and finally to building strengths and skills for optimal adjustment in the future.

The Workbook serves the following functions:

- It is an aid to focusing and directing the therapeutic process of critical incident stress debriefing.

- It is a medium for communication, introducing recall of the critical incidents or concerns in a safe, supportive setting.

- It invites the witness to explore the range of feelings, thoughts, and options.

- It serves as an assessment tool for the therapist, to help determine how the witness is integrating her experience.

- It can be used as a vehicle for educating the child about the issues surrounding the experience, and for helping him or her to develop the strengths and skills needed for successful mastery of a difficult life situation.

AN IMPORTANT NOTE

This Workbook, and all other Growth and Recovery Workbooks from Hunter House, are not self-help tools. They are intended to be used in the clinical setting by therapists, counselors, and school psychologists. Successful completion of the tasks in the workbook requires a sense of safety and support provided by the therapeutic alliance. The combination of a safe therapeutic relationship and a structured approach to debriefing provides the optimal opportunity for healing and recovery from trauma. Therefore, these Growth and Recovery Workbooks should not be given to guardians or parents to work through with their children in an unsupervised setting. The workbooks should not be given to children to take home until the therapeutic process is completed according to the therapist's standard of satisfaction.

PAGE-BY-PAGE DISCUSSION

For a more complete discussion of treatment considerations for children, see *Trauma in the Lives of Children by Kendall Johnson, Ph.D.* (Hunter House, Alameda, 1998). In the comments below, several tasks are specifically cross-referenced to discussions in that book, which is denoted TLC.

Pages 1–3 are introductory and trust building. They serve to establish and strengthen the therapeutic alliance, as well as to elicit important information regarding the child's frame of reference and self-image. It is important to make sure that this alliance is firmly established before moving on. Additional activities to support trust-building can include drawing a self-portrait, starting a self-identity collage using magazine pictures, reading a story together, or playing a trust-building game such as *The Ungame* or *The Self-Esteem Game*.

Page 1 initiates contact with the child in a non-threatening and personally empowering way, and communicates to the child that he or she is viewed as unique and special in the therapeutic environment.

Page 2 focuses on a discussion of self-worth and self-esteem. The child's responses to the list of important things about himself and his family measure his positive feelings and current affective state. If the child has difficulty with this task, he can return to it later. Returning to the task gives information about the child's progress and can be used

to validate the good feelings that develop as a result of the therapy.

Page 3 establishes the expectation for the book and for the course of therapy. The child is not viewed as a victim, but as a survivor, someone capable of successful adaptation to critical events. The child learns that therapy may be fun, but it is not play. This awareness heightens the child's ability to stay on task.

Pages 4 and 5 follow a progression from a "left-brain" written overview to the "right-brain" exercise of drawing the critical incident scene. The value of art therapies and artistic expression in establishing rapport, gaining access to unconscious material, and providing opportunities for the expression of unacceptable feelings is well-documented. *(Ref. TLC pages 142–146, 169–173)*

Pages 6–8 list incident-specific details designed to elicit the in-depth recall necessary for healing from trauma. The process follows the format used in critical incident stress debriefing and serves to defuse traumatic images which may be blocking the normal grief process. *(Ref. TLC pages 93–98)* Research in the fields of memory and trauma indicate that spontaneous memory recall is weak in young children. Children's memory for detail of significant events relies heavily on recognition recall, or being triggered to the relevant information. Further, research in the field of traumatology indicates that sensory details for critical incidents are stored separately within the brain structure and require a central trigger, or "file," to be recalled as relevant to a specific event. (*Ref. TLC pages 121–123*)

Page 9 lists some physical and affective symptoms experienced by victims of trauma during the critical event. The child's initial response to this task can be expanded after a trusting relationship has been established with the therapist. An expanded list of signs and symptoms of traumatic experience can be used to trigger more in-depth experiential memories. Such a list is found in *TLC on page 47.*

Page 10 provides the opportunity to transfer recall of the affective experience from left-to-right brain. Expression of feelings can also be augmented by other art activities, acting, sand tray work, or role-playing.

These pages provide a necessary opportunity for graphic and symbolic expression of the traumatic impressions. Lenore Terr's work with child survivors points to the use of symbolization and condensation as common posttraumatic responses. Variables which influence the symbolization process include background experiences and issues, developmental level of the child, and the circumstances surrounding the current event. (*Ref. TLC pages 62–65*) Terr also notes that separate ideas and images may be condensed in the symbolization process, requiring a careful sorting process during therapeutic intervention.

Pages 11–12 draw the survivor's attention to physical locations related to the incident and her associated reactions. She has the opportunity to explore her sense of safety in associated locations, to review her conclusions about how safe she is in the world, and to resolve issues of fear and distrust so that subsequent development will not be impeded.

Many diffuse posttraumatic symptoms can be traced to insecurity and a loss of sense of safety in familiar locations such as home, school, playground, and local stores. Additional work regarding restoration of feelings of safety and security in the environment are important in restoring the child to full function. Directions may be given to the survivor for drawing a map of the area in which the critical incident occurred. A floor plan may be used to elicit additional details regarding the event. Here again, triggers allow the child to access portions of the experience that have been recorded but that elude recall. The child may develop a three-dimensional model to use in this therapeutic

journey towards healing, or may opt to take a field trip to the location. The initial Workbook tasks serve as a springboard for these efforts. (*Ref. TLC pages 130–150*)

Pages 13–16 provide the opportunity to reveal trauma-specific information regarding other family members' experiences and their current condition. The intensity of the child's sense of responsibility for her family's safety can also reveal potentially damaging distortions regarding the child's sense of power and control in the world.

Page 17 addresses the child's actions and sense of responsibility during the event. A child has a natural egocentric sense of power that is easily magnified when, as a survivor, she experiences the helplessness that accompanies the inability to stop or change the course of events. The greater the sense of responsibility assumed by the child, the greater will be the traumatic impact. Appropriate placement of responsibility for events which are out of the child's control is crucial to provide the child with relief from her misplaced sense of guilt and obligation.

Pages 18 and 19 make the transition from memories to present reality and delayed reactions. Adequate time must be spent and collateral activities utilized to fully explore and defuse situations which might trigger fears, phobias, and anxiety reactions in the future. Assurance that reactions to recognition triggers of the critical event are normal is helpful, as are behavioral and cognitive behavior modification approaches to symptom relief. (*Ref. TLC pages 130–150*)

Finally, if anxiety or depressive symptoms are unmanageable and resistant to treatment, consideration of a psychiatric referral for medication is appropriate. (*Ref. TLC pages 150–152*)

Page 20 invites exploration of the survivor's "inner plan of action," which is the survivor's attempt to undo the event which has caused pain and stress. This rewriting of history is common in both child and adult survivors of trauma. Expanding this task can involve playing out, acting out, or taping the new script. Material related to the survivor's inner plan can also be utilized in family and group therapy. (*Ref. TLC pages 149–150, 156–158, 195–197*)

Page 21 addresses the child's experience of sharing the traumatic event with others. Victims who experience negative or nonresponsive reactions from others will find their healing process impeded. *TLC pages 283–284* provide a checklist for parental reactions to a child in crisis. TLC page 287–289 offers a discussion of the effects of parental reaction on young victims. This task can be extended by suggesting the survivor draw or write about each of the people he has talked with about the event, noting their reaction and how he would have liked to have responded to them. Puppets, toy animals, or the Gestalt Chair Method can then be utilized to augment the impact of the "rewriting of history." *(Ref. TLC pages 120–121, 138–139)*

Pages 22–23 provide both a cognitive and a projective assessment of the changes in self-concept which have occurred as a result of the traumatic incident. The loss of control experienced by victims of trauma contributes significantly to changes in self-image, often including a loss of self-confidence and self-esteem. Rebuilding a positive self-image is a crucial step in recovery from trauma.

Page 23 provides a description of the current state of the child's posttraumatic concept of self. The child has had the opportunity to debrief and to achieve a level of integration. This page uncovers enduring posttraumatic effects.

Pages 24–25 provide the opportunity to explore the child's dreams surrounding the critical event. Sleep disturbance, dreams, and nightmares are indicative of delayed stress reaction, and provide clues to the child's position in the posttraumatic stress cycle. *(Ref. TLC pages 15–16, 59–60)* The opportunity is provided to experience a sense of mastery over the feelings of helplessness which accompany nightmares and night terrors. Extended activities can include playing out dreams utilizing play or sand tray materials, writing new scripts for dreams, and analyzing dream material using gestalt dialogue techniques. *(Ref. TLC pages 138–149)*

Page 26 provides an opportunity to explore the more prominent or incongruent triggers associated with the event. If this effort at recall produces trauma-related affective responses, more work is needed to defuse sensory triggers and "stuck memories." The child's ability to identify a funny or exciting element of the traumatic event indicates progress has been made towards integration of the event into the larger context of the child's life.

Pages 27–32 facilitate a reorganization (Johnson calls it a "resorting") of the effects of the traumatic event. *TLC pages 120–121 and 154–156* describe the conceptual accommodations necessary for optimal integration. These pages utilize both written and projective means to access strengths and identify resources to be developed in recovery.

Keep in mind that the survivor is likely to recall new memories as recovering ego strength allows, particularly during the latter, empowerment stages of the therapeutic progression. These may be seen as setbacks because symptoms will temporarily reoccur. The therapist can be particularly helpful at this point, by providing perspective and hope.

Page 27 is an especially important strength building exercise in which the survivor identifies significant others in his support system. The list often includes new or different individuals than may have comprised the child's system of support prior to the critical incident. The child's need to identify whom to talk to is only the first step in the work. Most young people also need instruction in HOW to talk to others about sensitive topics. Extended activities that involve more specific identification and expression of feelings and practice dialogue are useful. *(Ref. TLC pages 154–156, 173–176)*

Pages 28–29 use the analogies of racing and sports to empower the child to a more assertive approach to life's events and challenges.

Pages 30–31 guide the survivor to see the positive growth and strength that can result from even the most catastrophic traumatic experiences. Recognition that crisis and trauma, while unwelcome, can have positive outcomes is critical to maintaining the survivor's optimism about the future.

Page 32 directs the child to a "positive perspective point." An important consideration for the termination of therapy is whether the child can identify strengths and positives in his or her current life situation. Here the child also has an opportunity to solidify a sense of positive power by identifying current resources and giving voices to wishes and hopes for the future.

We welcome comments on this guide and Workbook. To give suggestions for new Growth and Recovery Workbooks, or to order more Workbooks, call (800) 266-5592, fax (510) 865-4295, or write to:

Growth and Recovery Workbooks
c/o Hunter House Inc.
PO Box 2914
Alameda, California 94501-0914

GROWTH & RECOVERY WORKBOOKS
... helping and healing children ...

You are a
special person

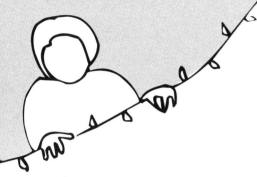

Write your name and
draw a picture of you here

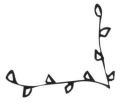

Write five important things you want people to know about you

_____

_____

_____

_____

_____

Write five things you want people to know about your home and family

_____

_____

_____

_____

_____

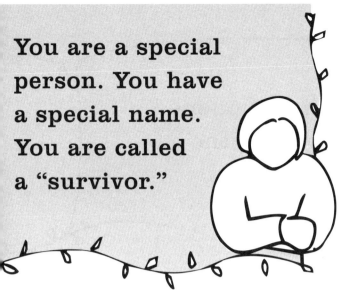

You are a special person. You have a special name. You are called a "survivor."

A survivor is someone who has been in something important, scary or exciting, like

- an accident

- a fire

- a hurricane

- an earthquake

- a flood

- or something else

This is your book. In it you can tell how you survived.

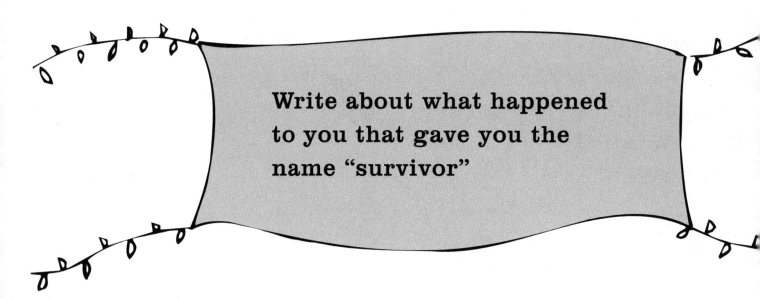

Write about what happened
to you that gave you the
name "survivor"

Draw a picture of what happened

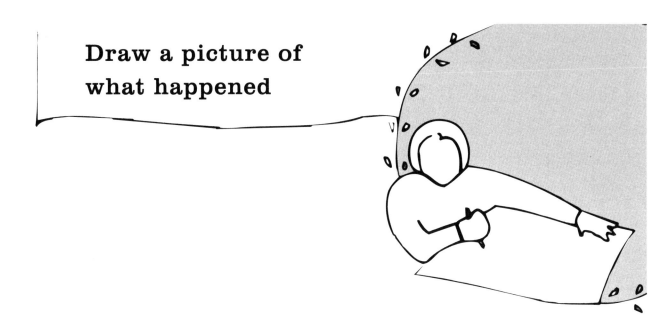

Sometimes it is hard to remember everything you saw or all the things that happened to you

This list may help you remember some of the things you saw and heard when you were a survivor. Check all the words that make you think about what happened:

- a house falling
- a helicopter
- people hurt
- water everywhere
- a bus
- a big boom
- fire
- glass breaking
- trees flying
- lots of wind

- the sidewalk cracking
- a broken bridge
- bodies
- a firefighter
- people screaming
- blood
- an airplane
- the beach
- a fast river

Write down any other words that remind you of what happened.

_____

_____

_____

Draw a picture of some scary things you saw

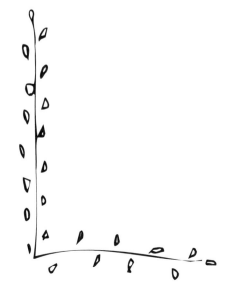

Draw a picture to show what
the noises sounded like

Here are some things survivors say they felt:

"I felt like running"

"My heart pounded out of my chest"

"I wanted to scream"

"I was excited"

"I was scared"

"I was angry"

"I didn't know what to do"

"My stomach hurt"

"I felt sweaty"

"Everything stopped"

"My head hurt"

Write how you felt when things were happening

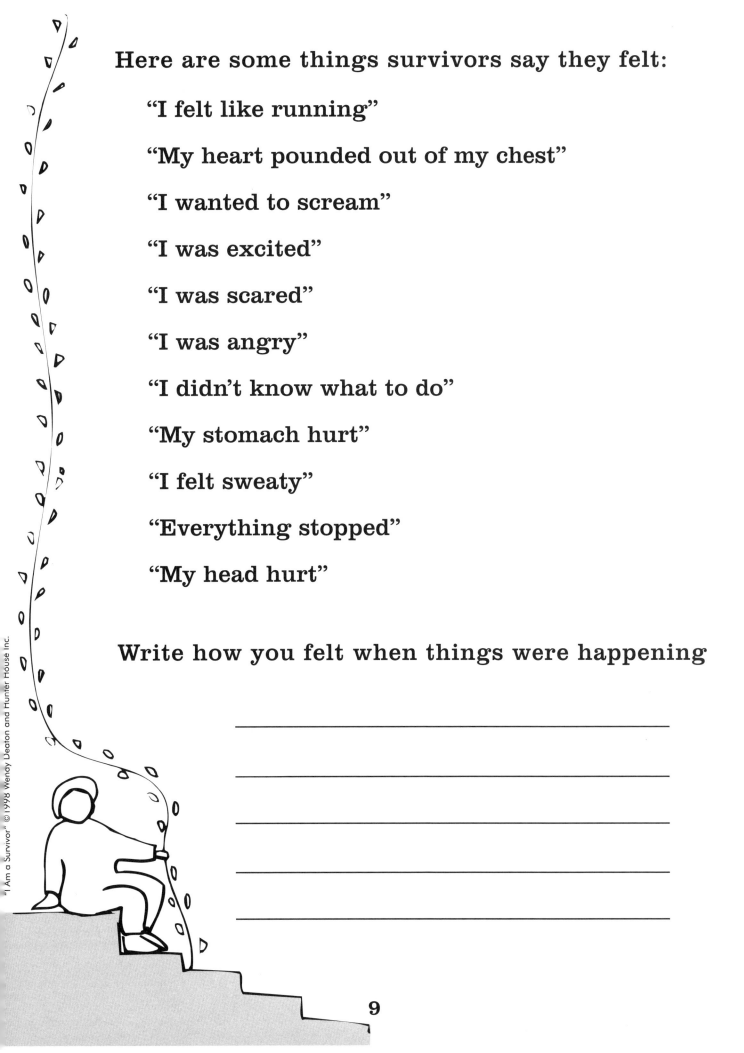

_____

_____

_____

_____

_____

Draw a picture to show how you felt

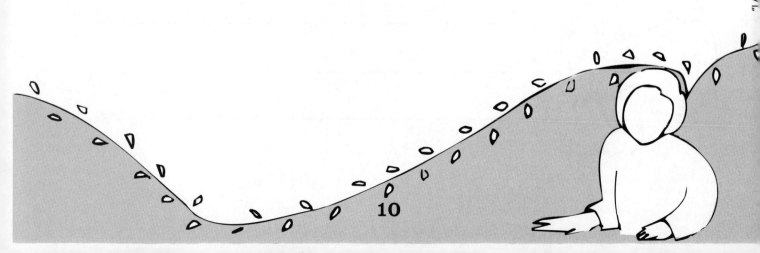

"I Am a Survivor" ©1998 Wendy Deaton and Hunter House Inc.

Something happened and you were there.
Where were you when it happened?

Write or tell how you feel about that place now

Do you feel safe in this place now?

Are there places you don't feel safe?
Check any places you don't feel safe

school	inside
stores	restaurants
cars	other houses
buses	your house
outside	near the water

Make a list of things you need to feel safe in these places

_____

_____

_____

_____

_____

_____

Who could you ask to help you plan how to feel safe?

_____

_____

_____

_____

_____

_____

_____

_____

_____

_____

_____

_____

_____

_____

_____

Where was your family when things were happening?

13

Did anything happen to anyone in your family or to a good friend?

Write about what happened

_____

_____

_____

_____

_____

_____

_____

_____

_____

_____

_____

Draw a picture of your family or your friends before anything happened

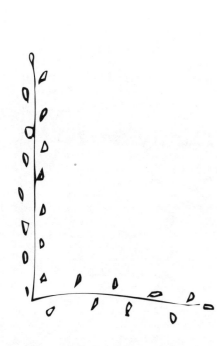

Some survivors feel as if what happened was their fault. They feel as if they caused it or should have been able to stop what happened.

Write about any feelings you have about it being your fault

_____

_____

_____

_____

_____

_____

What happened was not your fault. You were not responsible. If you have any of these feelings you need to forgive yourself for not being able to stop or change what happened.

Do some of these things bother you now?

- sudden noises
- the dark
- sirens
- helicopters
- the water
- going outside

- people yelling or crying
- being in a closed place
- things breaking
- cars or buses
- bright lights
- crowds of people

- anything else?

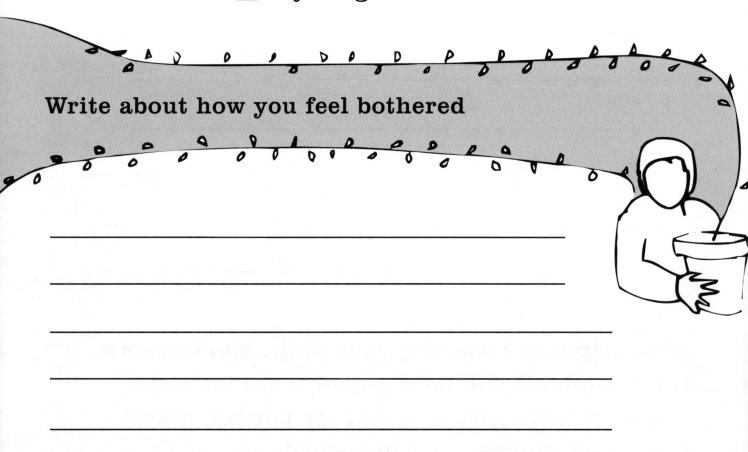

Write about how you feel bothered

_____

_____

_____

_____

_____

_____

Draw a picture of the worst thing you worry might happen

**Do you wish you could
change what happened?**

**Write or draw about what things
you would like to change**

Draw a picture of someone you told about what happened. Show how they looked when you told them. Show how you felt talking about what happened.

**Draw a picture of you before
you were a survivor**

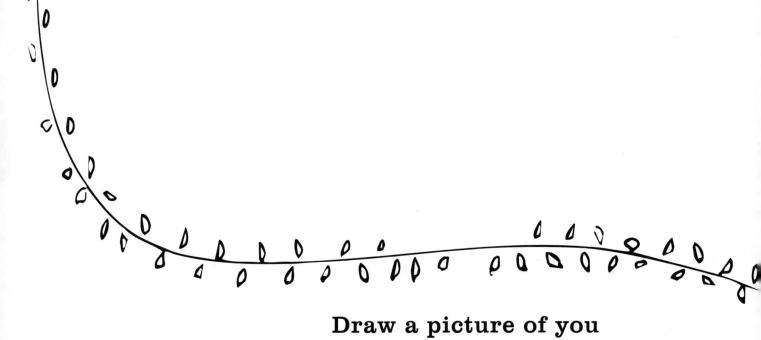

**Draw a picture of you
right after it happened**

Have you changed because of what happened?

Write or draw any changes that happened to you.

When scary things happen, you may
have bad dreams

Write about or draw a picture to
show any bad dreams you remember

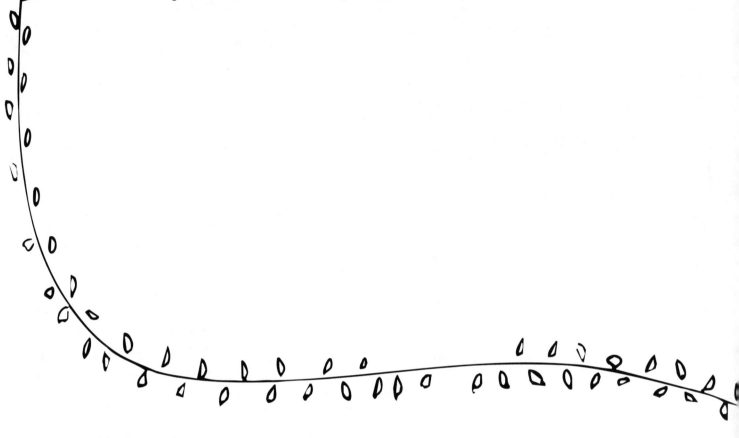

What do you do when you have a bad dream?

What are some things you could do to make
your dreams feel better?

_____

_____

_____

_____

**Write or draw a picture
of the kind of dreams you
would like to have**

What happened to you may have been scary or painful. Some things may have happened that were exciting, different, or funny.

Write about or draw a picture of something that happened that was exciting, different, or funny

Make a list of people you can talk to who can help you feel better about what happened

_____

_____

_____

_____

_____

_____

_____

_____

_____

If you were in a race what kind of race would it be?

- [ ] bike
- [ ] skis
- [ ] boat
- [ ] skates
- [ ] running
- [ ] horses
- [ ] motorcycle
- [ ] car
- [ ] skateboard

what else? _____

If you were playing a game or sport what would it be?

- [ ] soccer
- [ ] softball
- [ ] volleyball
- [ ] baseball
- [ ] basketball
- [ ] football

what else? _____

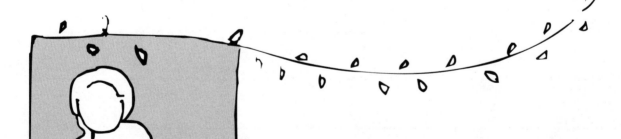

What are all the things you need to win?

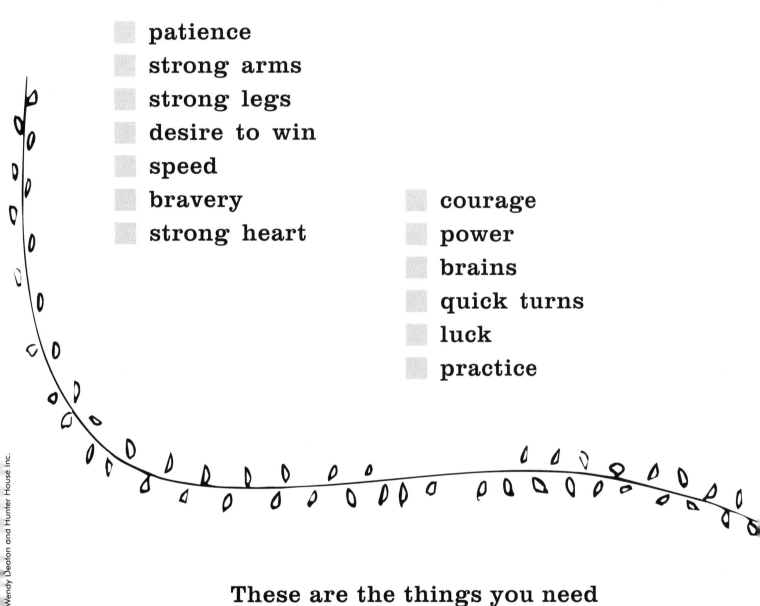

- patience
- strong arms
- strong legs
- desire to win
- speed
- bravery
- strong heart
- courage
- power
- brains
- quick turns
- luck
- practice

These are the things you need to feel strong and safe now

Write about something really good you learned from being a survivor

Make a list of things you can do to help you to survive if something else happens

_____

_____

_____

_____

_____

_____

_____

_____

_____

_____

_____

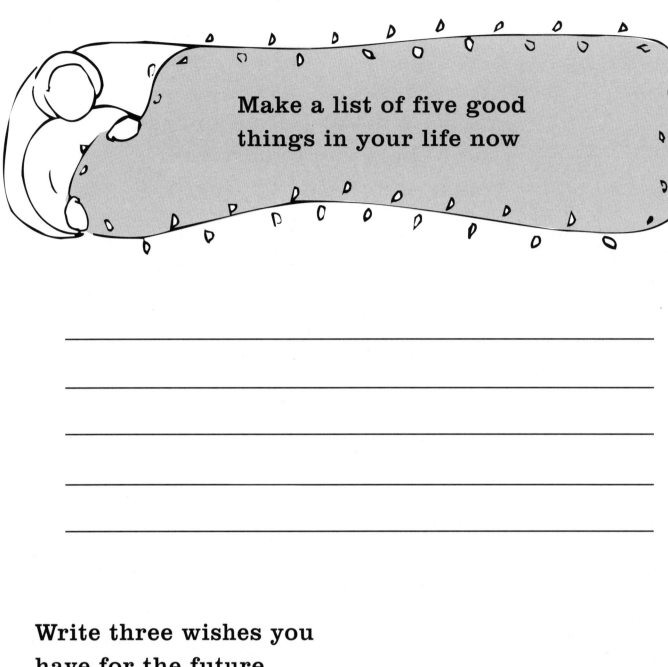

Make a list of five good things in your life now

_____

_____

_____

_____

_____

Write three wishes you have for the future

_____

_____

_____